A.C.T.S.

ADORATION * CONFESSION * THANKSGIVING * SUPPLICATION

Prayer Journal

DR. KARREN D. TODD

A.C.T.S. Prayer Journal
Adoration • Confession • Thanksgiving • Supplication

by Dr. Karren D. Todd

ISBN 978-1-7322339-2-8 (Paperback Edition)
Copyright © 2021 Karren D. Todd

All rights reserved. No part of this book may be reproduced in any form or by any electronic or mechanical means, including information storage and retrieval systems, without permission in writing from the publisher, except brief passages used in reviews.

First printing: June 2021

Editing by Sherronda Johnson
Cover design by K. Janey Media
Interior Journal design by Suzan David
Printed and bound in the United States of America

Unless indicated otherwise, Scripture references are from the New International Version.

Other Books by Dr. Todd
  Believe: God Can. God Will.
  One is a Whole Number: Recovering The Joy of Being Single
  Power Walk: 40 Day Journey to Power
  I'm Praying for You: A Collection of Life Giving Prayers

Published by Dr. Karren Todd
Memphis, TN USA 38116

Visit www.karrentodd.com

This journal belongs to:

_____

_____

_____

What is Prayer?

Prayer is the spiritual communication between humanity and God. It is a two-way dialogue that includes talking and listening. Prayer isn't a magical formula for getting what we want, and it isn't reserved for "holy" people, or for special times or places.

It is simply a conversation with God.

Prayer has always been a topic that either frees people or freezes people. We often look at the believers who flow effortlessly in prayer with one of two reactions: inspiration or intimidation. This journal is designed to take the intimidation out of prayer.

If you are a seasoned intercessor, you can add this model to your prayer and devotion time. If you are new to prayer, begin your journey here and watch your prayer life grow as you practice the ACTS of Prayer.

How to Use this Journal

Each day consists of two sections.

In the morning, craft your prayer for the day using the ACTS model. Once you have placed your sentences or thoughts in each element – pull them together and write out a complete prayer.

In the evening, revisit your journal to note the things that happened during your day that you are grateful for and then set your intentions for the next day. This space allows you to slow down, recover, and set yourself up for a powerful tomorrow.

Don't forget to go back and mark your answered prayers as God responds to your requests. This way you can pick up your journal at any time and see how God has moved in your life. You LITERALLY are keeping your "prayer receipts" in your journal.

The A.C.T.S. of Prayer

The Elements

Adoration
Giving God praise and honor for who God is as Divine Creator and Lord over all.

The first element of prayer should be **adoration or praise**. Adoration is perhaps the highest type of worship and is covered with an attitude of worship, love, and reverence towards God. As believers continue to mature in their faith and in the practice of prayer, more and more time is spent on this aspect of prayer

> *Yours, Lord, is the greatness and the power*
> *and the glory and the majesty and the splendor,*
> *for everything in heaven and earth is yours.*
> *Yours, Lord, is the kingdom;*
> *you are exalted as head over all.*
> *-1 Chronicles 29:11*

What Adoration/Praise looks like:
> God, I bless Your Holy Name...
> You are a Sovereign God who knows the beginning from the ending...
> To the one true and living God...
> You are altogether lovely. You are altogether wonderful.
> There is no God like You...

Confession
Honestly dealing with sin in your life.

Second, prayer should include **confession** as an acknowledgment of sin to God. Confession is being honest and transparent before God. It aligns what we say and do with what God desires of us. Each time we enter into God's presence through prayer we must acknowledge that we have sinned and fallen short of God's perfect glory.

Confession is not the same as asking for forgiveness; however, when we confess our sins there should be an implication that there will be a change of conduct or course of action on the part of the believer. It is ALWAYS appropriate to ask for forgiveness after confession.

> *If we confess our sins, he is faithful and just and will forgive us our sins and purify us from all unrighteousness. -1 John 1:9*
>
> *Whoever conceals their sins does not prosper,*
>   *but the one who confesses and renounces them finds mercy.*
> *-Proverbs 28:13*

What Confession looks like:
    God, I confess my sins to you...
    God, I repent for _____ and ask for Your forgiveness...
    God, I confess my shortcomings and every imperfection
    in light of Your perfect will...

Thanksgiving

Verbalizing what you're grateful for in your life and in the world around you.

Third, when we pray, we should always give **thanks**, remembering the grace and mercy God has shown toward us. As we ground our prayers in gratitude, we prepare our hearts for God's will and God's response.

> *Rejoice always, pray continually, give thanks in all circumstances; for this is God's will for you in Christ Jesus. -1 Thessalonians 5:16-18*
>
> *Enter his gates with thanksgiving and his courts with praise;*
> *give thanks to him and praise his name. -Psalm 100:4*

What Thanksgiving looks like:
    God, I thank You for...
    I praise You for You have done marvelous things...
    When I think about the times You _____ my heart overflows
    with thanksgiving...

Supplication

Praying for the needs of others and yourself.

Fourth, prayer includes **supplication or petition.** This is the time when we present our requests for ourselves and on behalf of others.

> *Do not be anxious about anything, but in every situation, by prayer and petition, with thanksgiving, present your requests to God. And the peace of God, which transcends all understanding, will guard your hearts and your minds in Christ Jesus. -Philippians 4:6-7*

> *And pray in the Spirit on all occasions with all kinds of prayers and requests. With this in mind, be alert and always keep on praying for all the Lord's people. -Ephesians 6:18*

What Supplication looks like:
- God, I ask that You…
- God, Your word says to make our requests known…
- God, I need You to/for…
- I am believing Your word that the effective, fervent prayers of the righteous avail much. Today I am praying for…

Bonus Elements

Closing Your Prayer

There's no "incorrect" way to close your prayer. However, there are several scriptures that encourage us to ask in Jesus' name (John 14:13-14; John 16:24; John 15:16; Col 3:17). So, as Christians, we do that most often.

Here are other suggestions:
- "In Jesus' name, I pray..."
- "In Your Holy Name"
- "Amen."
- "Thank You."
- "By Your power and might."
- "According to Your will."
- "For Your Glory.."
- "I pray this trusting and believing in You, Amen."

Your Prayer Voice

Talk to God in your regular voice. God is confident in two things: who God is and who you are. God hears your heart when you talk as you would a friend. Knowing every scripture and the newest Christian tag lines are not necessary. Just talk.

God is an ever-present God. This means that God is always with you – patiently waiting, always listening. If you need to talk to God daily, hourly, or minute-by-minute, do it.

Developing the Habit of Praying

1. Prioritize the Time.
2. Make a Plan.
3. Start the conversation.
4. Open your heart and ears to listen.
5. Sprinkle prayer throughout your day.

Today's A.C.T.S.

Date _____

Adoration
Giving God praise and honor for who God is as Divine Creator and Lord over all.

Confession
Honestly dealing with sin in your life.

Thanksgiving
Verbalizing what you're grateful for in your life and in the world around you.

Supplication
Praying for the needs of others and yourself.

Requests for myself	Answered
Requests for others	

Your Morning Prayer

Evening Reflection

I'm grateful for...

Three things I want to accomplish tomorrow...

Today's A.C.T.S.

Date _____

Adoration
Giving God praise and honor for who God is as Divine Creator and Lord over all.

Confession
Honestly dealing with sin in your life.

Thanksgiving
Verbalizing what you're grateful for in your life and in the world around you.

Supplication
Praying for the needs of others and yourself.

Requests for myself	Answered
Requests for others	

Your Morning Prayer

Evening Reflection
I'M GRATEFUL FOR...

THREE THINGS I WANT TO ACCOMPLISH TOMORROW...

Today's A.C.T.S.

Date _____

Adoration
Giving God praise and honor for who God is as Divine Creator and Lord over all.

Confession
Honestly dealing with sin in your life.

Thanksgiving
Verbalizing what you're grateful for in your life and in the world around you.

Supplication
Praying for the needs of others and yourself.

Requests for myself	Answered

Requests for others	

Your Morning Prayer

Evening Reflection

I'm grateful for...

Three things I want to accomplish tomorrow...

Today's A.C.T.S.

Date _____

Adoration
Giving God praise and honor for who God is as Divine Creator and Lord over all.

Confession
Honestly dealing with sin in your life.

Thanksgiving
Verbalizing what you're grateful for in your life and in the world around you.

Supplication
Praying for the needs of others and yourself.

Requests for myself	Answered

Requests for others	

Your Morning Prayer

Evening Reflection

I'm grateful for...

Three things I want to accomplish tomorrow...

Today's A.C.T.S.

Date _____

Adoration
Giving God praise and honor for who God is as Divine Creator and Lord over all.

Confession
Honestly dealing with sin in your life.

Thanksgiving
Verbalizing what you're grateful for in your life and in the world around you.

Supplication
Praying for the needs of others and yourself.

Requests for myself	Answered
Requests for others	

Your Morning Prayer

Evening Reflection

I'm grateful for...

Three things I want to accomplish tomorrow...

Today's A.C.T.S.

Date _____

Adoration
Giving God praise and honor for who God is as Divine Creator and Lord over all.

Confession
Honestly dealing with sin in your life.

Thanksgiving
Verbalizing what you're grateful for in your life and in the world around you.

Supplication
Praying for the needs of others and yourself.

Requests for myself	Answered
Requests for others	

Your Morning Prayer

Evening Reflection

I'M GRATEFUL FOR...

THREE THINGS I WANT TO ACCOMPLISH TOMORROW...

Today's A.C.T.S.

Date _____

Adoration
Giving God praise and honor for who God is as Divine Creator and Lord over all.

Confession
Honestly dealing with sin in your life.

Thanksgiving
Verbalizing what you're grateful for in your life and in the world around you.

Supplication
Praying for the needs of others and yourself.

Requests for myself	Answered

Requests for others	

Your Morning Prayer

Evening Reflection
I'm grateful for...

THREE THINGS I WANT TO ACCOMPLISH TOMORROW...

Today's A.C.T.S.

Date _____

Adoration
Giving God praise and honor for who God is as Divine Creator and Lord over all.

Confession
Honestly dealing with sin in your life.

Thanksgiving
Verbalizing what you're grateful for in your life and in the world around you.

Supplication
Praying for the needs of others and yourself.

Requests for myself	Answered

Requests for others	

Your Morning Prayer

Evening Reflection
I'm grateful for...

Three things I want to accomplish tomorrow...

Today's A.C.T.S.

Date _____

Adoration
Giving God praise and honor for who God is as Divine Creator and Lord over all.

Confession
Honestly dealing with sin in your life.

Thanksgiving
Verbalizing what you're grateful for in your life and in the world around you.

Supplication
Praying for the needs of others and yourself.

Requests for myself	Answered
Requests for others	

Your Morning Prayer

Evening Reflection

I'M GRATEFUL FOR...

THREE THINGS I WANT TO ACCOMPLISH TOMORROW...

Today's A.C.T.S.

Date _____

Adoration
Giving God praise and honor for who God is as Divine Creator and Lord over all.

Confession
Honestly dealing with sin in your life.

Thanksgiving
Verbalizing what you're grateful for in your life and in the world around you.

Supplication
Praying for the needs of others and yourself.

Requests for myself	Answered

Requests for others	

Your Morning Prayer

Evening Reflection

I'm grateful for...

Three things I want to accomplish tomorrow...

Today's A.C.T.S.

Date _____

Adoration
Giving God praise and honor for who God is as Divine Creator and Lord over all.

Confession
Honestly dealing with sin in your life.

Thanksgiving
Verbalizing what you're grateful for in your life and in the world around you.

Supplication
Praying for the needs of others and yourself.

Requests for myself	Answered
Requests for others	

Your Morning Prayer

Evening Reflection

I'm grateful for...

Three things I want to accomplish tomorrow...

Today's A.C.T.S.

Date _____

Adoration
Giving God praise and honor for who God is as Divine Creator and Lord over all.

Confession
Honestly dealing with sin in your life.

Thanksgiving
Verbalizing what you're grateful for in your life and in the world around you.

Supplication
Praying for the needs of others and yourself.

Requests for myself	Answered
Requests for others	

Your Morning Prayer

Evening Reflection

I'm grateful for...

Three things I want to accomplish tomorrow...

Today's A.C.T.S.

Date _____

Adoration
Giving God praise and honor for who God is as Divine Creator and Lord over all.

Confession
Honestly dealing with sin in your life.

Thanksgiving
Verbalizing what you're grateful for in your life and in the world around you.

Supplication
Praying for the needs of others and yourself.

Requests for myself	Answered
Requests for others	

Your Morning Prayer

Evening Reflection
I'm grateful for...

Three things I want to accomplish tomorrow...

Today's A.C.T.S.

Date _____

Adoration
Giving God praise and honor for who God is as Divine Creator and Lord over all.

Confession
Honestly dealing with sin in your life.

Thanksgiving
Verbalizing what you're grateful for in your life and in the world around you.

Supplication
Praying for the needs of others and yourself.

Requests for myself	Answered
Requests for others	

Your Morning Prayer

Evening Reflection

I'm grateful for...

Three things I want to accomplish tomorrow...

Today's A.C.T.S.

Date _____

Adoration
Giving God praise and honor for who God is as Divine Creator and Lord over all.

Confession
Honestly dealing with sin in your life.

Thanksgiving
Verbalizing what you're grateful for in your life and in the world around you.

Supplication
Praying for the needs of others and yourself.

Requests for myself	Answered
Requests for others	

Your Morning Prayer

Evening Reflection

I'M GRATEFUL FOR...

THREE THINGS I WANT TO ACCOMPLISH TOMORROW...

Today's A.C.T.S.

Date _____

Adoration
Giving God praise and honor for who God is as Divine Creator and Lord over all.

Confession
Honestly dealing with sin in your life.

Thanksgiving
Verbalizing what you're grateful for in your life and in the world around you.

Supplication
Praying for the needs of others and yourself.

Requests for myself	Answered
Requests for others	

Your Morning Prayer

Evening Reflection

I'm grateful for...

Three things I want to accomplish tomorrow...

Today's A.C.T.S.

Date _____

Adoration
Giving God praise and honor for who God is as Divine Creator and Lord over all.

Confession
Honestly dealing with sin in your life.

Thanksgiving
Verbalizing what you're grateful for in your life and in the world around you.

Supplication
Praying for the needs of others and yourself.

Requests for myself	Answered
Requests for others	

Your Morning Prayer

Evening Reflection
I'm grateful for...

Three things I want to accomplish tomorrow...

Today's A.C.T.S.

Date _____

Adoration
Giving God praise and honor for who God is as Divine Creator and Lord over all.

Confession
Honestly dealing with sin in your life.

Thanksgiving
Verbalizing what you're grateful for in your life and in the world around you.

Supplication
Praying for the needs of others and yourself.

Requests for myself	Answered

Requests for others	

Your Morning Prayer

Evening Reflection
I'm grateful for...

Three things I want to accomplish tomorrow...

Today's A.C.T.S.

Date _____

Adoration
Giving God praise and honor for who God is as Divine Creator and Lord over all.

Confession
Honestly dealing with sin in your life.

Thanksgiving
Verbalizing what you're grateful for in your life and in the world around you.

Supplication
Praying for the needs of others and yourself.

Requests for myself	Answered
Requests for others	

Your Morning Prayer

Evening Reflection

I'm grateful for...

Three things I want to accomplish tomorrow...

Today's A.C.T.S.

Date _____

Adoration
Giving God praise and honor for who God is as Divine Creator and Lord over all.

Confession
Honestly dealing with sin in your life.

Thanksgiving
Verbalizing what you're grateful for in your life and in the world around you.

Supplication
Praying for the needs of others and yourself.

Requests for myself	Answered
Requests for others	

Your Morning Prayer

Evening Reflection
I'm grateful for...

Three things I want to accomplish tomorrow...

Today's A.C.T.S.

Date _____

Adoration
Giving God praise and honor for who God is as Divine Creator and Lord over all.

Confession
Honestly dealing with sin in your life.

Thanksgiving
Verbalizing what you're grateful for in your life and in the world around you.

Supplication
Praying for the needs of others and yourself.

Requests for myself	Answered
Requests for others	

Your Morning Prayer

Evening Reflection

I'm grateful for...

Three things I want to accomplish tomorrow...

Today's A.C.T.S.

Date _____

Adoration
Giving God praise and honor for who God is as Divine Creator and Lord over all.

Confession
Honestly dealing with sin in your life.

Thanksgiving
Verbalizing what you're grateful for in your life and in the world around you.

Supplication
Praying for the needs of others and yourself.

Requests for myself	Answered
Requests for others	

Your Morning Prayer

Evening Reflection

I'm grateful for...

THREE THINGS I WANT TO ACCOMPLISH TOMORROW...

Today's A.C.T.S.

Date _____

Adoration
Giving God praise and honor for who God is as Divine Creator and Lord over all.

Confession
Honestly dealing with sin in your life.

Thanksgiving
Verbalizing what you're grateful for in your life and in the world around you.

Supplication
Praying for the needs of others and yourself.

Requests for myself	Answered
Requests for others	

Your Morning Prayer

Evening Reflection

I'm grateful for...

Three things I want to accomplish tomorrow...

Today's A.C.T.S.

Date _____

Adoration
Giving God praise and honor for who God is as Divine Creator and Lord over all.

Confession
Honestly dealing with sin in your life.

Thanksgiving
Verbalizing what you're grateful for in your life and in the world around you.

Supplication
Praying for the needs of others and yourself.

Requests for myself	Answered

Requests for others	

Your Morning Prayer

Evening Reflection
I'm grateful for...

Three things I want to accomplish tomorrow...

Today's A.C.T.S.

Date _____

Adoration
Giving God praise and honor for who God is as Divine Creator and Lord over all.

Confession
Honestly dealing with sin in your life.

Thanksgiving
Verbalizing what you're grateful for in your life and in the world around you.

Supplication
Praying for the needs of others and yourself.

Requests for myself	Answered

Requests for others	

Your Morning Prayer

Evening Reflection

I'm grateful for...

Three things I want to accomplish tomorrow...

Today's A.C.T.S.

Date _____

Adoration
Giving God praise and honor for who God is as Divine Creator and Lord over all.

Confession
Honestly dealing with sin in your life.

Thanksgiving
Verbalizing what you're grateful for in your life and in the world around you.

Supplication
Praying for the needs of others and yourself.

Requests for myself	Answered
Requests for others	

Your Morning Prayer

Evening Reflection

I'm grateful for...

Three things I want to accomplish tomorrow...

Today's A.C.T.S.

Date _____

Adoration
Giving God praise and honor for who God is as Divine Creator and Lord over all.

Confession
Honestly dealing with sin in your life.

Thanksgiving
Verbalizing what you're grateful for in your life and in the world around you.

Supplication
Praying for the needs of others and yourself.

Requests for myself	Answered
Requests for others	

Your Morning Prayer

Evening Reflection

I'm grateful for...

Three things I want to accomplish tomorrow...

Today's A.C.T.S.

Date _____

Adoration
Giving God praise and honor for who God is as Divine Creator and Lord over all.

Confession
Honestly dealing with sin in your life.

Thanksgiving
Verbalizing what you're grateful for in your life and in the world around you.

Supplication
Praying for the needs of others and yourself.

Requests for myself	Answered
Requests for others	

Your Morning Prayer

Evening Reflection

I'M GRATEFUL FOR...

THREE THINGS I WANT TO ACCOMPLISH TOMORROW...

Today's A.C.T.S.

Date _____

Adoration
Giving God praise and honor for who God is as Divine Creator and Lord over all.

Confession
Honestly dealing with sin in your life.

Thanksgiving
Verbalizing what you're grateful for in your life and in the world around you.

Supplication
Praying for the needs of others and yourself.

Requests for myself	Answered
Requests for others	

Your Morning Prayer

Evening Reflection

I'm grateful for...

Three things I want to accomplish tomorrow...

Today's A.C.T.S.

Date _____

Adoration
Giving God praise and honor for who God is as Divine Creator and Lord over all.

Confession
Honestly dealing with sin in your life.

Thanksgiving
Verbalizing what you're grateful for in your life and in the world around you.

Supplication
Praying for the needs of others and yourself.

Requests for myself	Answered
Requests for others	

Your Morning Prayer

Evening Reflection
I'M GRATEFUL FOR...

THREE THINGS I WANT TO ACCOMPLISH TOMORROW...

Today's A.C.T.S.

Date _____

Adoration
Giving God praise and honor for who God is as Divine Creator and Lord over all.

Confession
Honestly dealing with sin in your life.

Thanksgiving
Verbalizing what you're grateful for in your life and in the world around you.

Supplication
Praying for the needs of others and yourself.

Requests for myself	Answered
Requests for others	

Your Morning Prayer

Evening Reflection

I'M GRATEFUL FOR...

THREE THINGS I WANT TO ACCOMPLISH TOMORROW...

Today's A.C.T.S.

Date _____

Adoration
Giving God praise and honor for who God is as Divine Creator and Lord over all.

Confession
Honestly dealing with sin in your life.

Thanksgiving
Verbalizing what you're grateful for in your life and in the world around you.

Supplication
Praying for the needs of others and yourself.

Requests for myself	Answered
Requests for others	

Your Morning Prayer

Evening Reflection

I'm grateful for...

Three things I want to accomplish tomorrow...

Today's A.C.T.S.

Date _____

Adoration
Giving God praise and honor for who God is as Divine Creator and Lord over all.

Confession
Honestly dealing with sin in your life.

Thanksgiving
Verbalizing what you're grateful for in your life and in the world around you.

Supplication
Praying for the needs of others and yourself.

Requests for myself	Answered
Requests for others	

Your Morning Prayer

Evening Reflection

I'm grateful for...

Three things I want to accomplish tomorrow...

Today's A.C.T.S.

Date _____

Adoration
Giving God praise and honor for who God is as Divine Creator and Lord over all.

Confession
Honestly dealing with sin in your life.

Thanksgiving
Verbalizing what you're grateful for in your life and in the world around you.

Supplication
Praying for the needs of others and yourself.

Requests for myself	Answered
Requests for others	

Your Morning Prayer

Evening Reflection

I'm grateful for...

Three things I want to accomplish tomorrow...

Today's A.C.T.S.

Date _____

Adoration
Giving God praise and honor for who God is as Divine Creator and Lord over all.

Confession
Honestly dealing with sin in your life.

Thanksgiving
Verbalizing what you're grateful for in your life and in the world around you.

Supplication
Praying for the needs of others and yourself.

Requests for myself	Answered
Requests for others	

Your Morning Prayer

Evening Reflection
I'm grateful for...

Three things I want to accomplish tomorrow...

Today's A.C.T.S.

Date _____

Adoration
Giving God praise and honor for who God is as Divine Creator and Lord over all.

Confession
Honestly dealing with sin in your life.

Thanksgiving
Verbalizing what you're grateful for in your life and in the world around you.

Supplication
Praying for the needs of others and yourself.

Requests for myself	Answered

Requests for others

Your Morning Prayer

Evening Reflection

I'm grateful for...

Three things I want to accomplish tomorrow...

Today's A.C.T.S.

Date _____

Adoration
Giving God praise and honor for who God is as Divine Creator and Lord over all.

Confession
Honestly dealing with sin in your life.

Thanksgiving
Verbalizing what you're grateful for in your life and in the world around you.

Supplication
Praying for the needs of others and yourself.

Requests for myself	Answered
Requests for others	

Your Morning Prayer

Evening Reflection
I'm grateful for...

Three things I want to accomplish tomorrow...

Today's A.C.T.S.

Date _____

Adoration
Giving God praise and honor for who God is as Divine Creator and Lord over all.

Confession
Honestly dealing with sin in your life.

Thanksgiving
Verbalizing what you're grateful for in your life and in the world around you.

Supplication
Praying for the needs of others and yourself.

Requests for myself	Answered
Requests for others	

Your Morning Prayer

Evening Reflection

I'm grateful for...

Three things I want to accomplish tomorrow...

Today's A.C.T.S.

Date _____

Adoration
Giving God praise and honor for who God is as Divine Creator and Lord over all.

Confession
Honestly dealing with sin in your life.

Thanksgiving
Verbalizing what you're grateful for in your life and in the world around you.

Supplication
Praying for the needs of others and yourself.

Requests for myself	Answered
Requests for others	

Your Morning Prayer

Evening Reflection
I'm grateful for...

Three things I want to accomplish tomorrow...

Today's A.C.T.S.

Date _____

Adoration
Giving God praise and honor for who God is as Divine Creator and Lord over all.

Confession
Honestly dealing with sin in your life.

Thanksgiving
Verbalizing what you're grateful for in your life and in the world around you.

Supplication
Praying for the needs of others and yourself.

Requests for myself	Answered
Requests for others	

Your Morning Prayer

Evening Reflection

I'm grateful for...

Three things I want to accomplish tomorrow...

Today's A.C.T.S.

Date _____

Adoration
Giving God praise and honor for who God is as Divine Creator and Lord over all.

Confession
Honestly dealing with sin in your life.

Thanksgiving
Verbalizing what you're grateful for in your life and in the world around you.

Supplication
Praying for the needs of others and yourself.

Requests for myself	Answered
Requests for others	

Your Morning Prayer

Evening Reflection
I'm grateful for...

THREE THINGS I WANT TO ACCOMPLISH TOMORROW...

Today's A.C.T.S.

Date _____

Adoration
Giving God praise and honor for who God is as Divine Creator and Lord over all.

Confession
Honestly dealing with sin in your life.

Thanksgiving
Verbalizing what you're grateful for in your life and in the world around you.

Supplication
Praying for the needs of others and yourself.

Requests for myself	Answered

Requests for others

Your Morning Prayer

Evening Reflection
I'm grateful for...

Three things I want to accomplish tomorrow...

Today's A.C.T.S.

Date _____

Adoration
Giving God praise and honor for who God is as Divine Creator and Lord over all.

Confession
Honestly dealing with sin in your life.

Thanksgiving
Verbalizing what you're grateful for in your life and in the world around you.

Supplication
Praying for the needs of others and yourself.

Requests for myself	Answered
Requests for others	

Your Morning Prayer

Evening Reflection
I'm grateful for...

Three things I want to accomplish tomorrow...

Today's A.C.T.S.

Date _____

Adoration
Giving God praise and honor for who God is as Divine Creator and Lord over all.

Confession
Honestly dealing with sin in your life.

Thanksgiving
Verbalizing what you're grateful for in your life and in the world around you.

Supplication
Praying for the needs of others and yourself.

Requests for myself	Answered
Requests for others	

Your Morning Prayer

Evening Reflection

I'm grateful for...

THREE THINGS I WANT TO ACCOMPLISH TOMORROW...

Today's A.C.T.S.

Date _____

Adoration
Giving God praise and honor for who God is as Divine Creator and Lord over all.

Confession
Honestly dealing with sin in your life.

Thanksgiving
Verbalizing what you're grateful for in your life and in the world around you.

Supplication
Praying for the needs of others and yourself.

Requests for myself	Answered
Requests for others	

Your Morning Prayer

Evening Reflection

I'm grateful for...

Three things I want to accomplish tomorrow...

Today's A.C.T.S.

Date _____

Adoration
Giving God praise and honor for who God is as Divine Creator and Lord over all.

Confession
Honestly dealing with sin in your life.

Thanksgiving
Verbalizing what you're grateful for in your life and in the world around you.

Supplication
Praying for the needs of others and yourself.

Requests for myself	Answered

Requests for others

Your Morning Prayer

Evening Reflection

I'm grateful for...

Three things I want to accomplish tomorrow...

Today's A.C.T.S.

Date _____

Adoration
Giving God praise and honor for who God is as Divine Creator and Lord over all.

Confession
Honestly dealing with sin in your life.

Thanksgiving
Verbalizing what you're grateful for in your life and in the world around you.

Supplication
Praying for the needs of others and yourself.

Requests for myself	Answered
Requests for others	

Your Morning Prayer

Evening Reflection

I'm grateful for...

Three things I want to accomplish tomorrow...

Today's A.C.T.S.

Date _____

Adoration
Giving God praise and honor for who God is as Divine Creator and Lord over all.

Confession
Honestly dealing with sin in your life.

Thanksgiving
Verbalizing what you're grateful for in your life and in the world around you.

Supplication
Praying for the needs of others and yourself.

Requests for myself	Answered
Requests for others	

Your Morning Prayer

Evening Reflection
I'm grateful for...

Three things I want to accomplish tomorrow...

Today's A.C.T.S.

Date _____

Adoration
Giving God praise and honor for who God is as Divine Creator and Lord over all.

Confession
Honestly dealing with sin in your life.

Thanksgiving
Verbalizing what you're grateful for in your life and in the world around you.

Supplication
Praying for the needs of others and yourself.

Requests for myself	Answered
Requests for others	

Your Morning Prayer

Evening Reflection
I'm grateful for...

Three things I want to accomplish tomorrow...

Today's A.C.T.S.

Date _____

Adoration

Giving God praise and honor for who God is as Divine Creator and Lord over all.

Confession

Honestly dealing with sin in your life.

Thanksgiving

Verbalizing what you're grateful for in your life and in the world around you.

Supplication

Praying for the needs of others and yourself.

Requests for myself	Answered
Requests for others	

Your Morning Prayer

Evening Reflection

I'm grateful for...

Three things I want to accomplish tomorrow...

Today's A.C.T.S.

Date _____

Adoration
Giving God praise and honor for who God is as Divine Creator and Lord over all.

Confession
Honestly dealing with sin in your life.

Thanksgiving
Verbalizing what you're grateful for in your life and in the world around you.

Supplication
Praying for the needs of others and yourself.

Requests for myself	Answered

Requests for others

Your Morning Prayer

Evening Reflection

I'm grateful for...

Three things I want to accomplish tomorrow...

Today's A.C.T.S.

Date _____

Adoration
Giving God praise and honor for who God is as Divine Creator and Lord over all.

Confession
Honestly dealing with sin in your life.

Thanksgiving
Verbalizing what you're grateful for in your life and in the world around you.

Supplication
Praying for the needs of others and yourself.

Requests for myself	Answered
Requests for others	

Your Morning Prayer

Evening Reflection
I'm grateful for...

THREE THINGS I WANT TO ACCOMPLISH TOMORROW...

Today's A.C.T.S.

Date _____

Adoration
Giving God praise and honor for who God is as Divine Creator and Lord over all.

Confession
Honestly dealing with sin in your life.

Thanksgiving
Verbalizing what you're grateful for in your life and in the world around you.

Supplication
Praying for the needs of others and yourself.

Requests for myself	Answered
Requests for others	

Your Morning Prayer

Evening Reflection

I'm grateful for...

Three things I want to accomplish tomorrow...

Today's A.C.T.S.

Date _____

Adoration
Giving God praise and honor for who God is as Divine Creator and Lord over all.

Confession
Honestly dealing with sin in your life.

Thanksgiving
Verbalizing what you're grateful for in your life and in the world around you.

Supplication
Praying for the needs of others and yourself.

Requests for myself	Answered
Requests for others	

Your Morning Prayer

Evening Reflection
I'm grateful for...

Three things I want to accomplish tomorrow...

Today's A.C.T.S.

Date _____

Adoration
Giving God praise and honor for who God is as Divine Creator and Lord over all.

Confession
Honestly dealing with sin in your life.

Thanksgiving
Verbalizing what you're grateful for in your life and in the world around you.

Supplication
Praying for the needs of others and yourself.

Requests for myself	Answered
Requests for others	

Your Morning Prayer

Evening Reflection

I'm grateful for...

Three things I want to accomplish tomorrow...

Today's A.C.T.S.

Date _____

Adoration
Giving God praise and honor for who God is as Divine Creator and Lord over all.

Confession
Honestly dealing with sin in your life.

Thanksgiving
Verbalizing what you're grateful for in your life and in the world around you.

Supplication
Praying for the needs of others and yourself.

Requests for myself	Answered
Requests for others	

Your Morning Prayer

Evening Reflection

I'm grateful for...

Three things I want to accomplish tomorrow...

Today's A.C.T.S.

Date _____

Adoration
Giving God praise and honor for who God is as Divine Creator and Lord over all.

Confession
Honestly dealing with sin in your life.

Thanksgiving
Verbalizing what you're grateful for in your life and in the world around you.

Supplication
Praying for the needs of others and yourself.

Requests for myself	Answered
Requests for others	

Your Morning Prayer

Evening Reflection

I'm grateful for...

Three things I want to accomplish tomorrow...

Today's A.C.T.S.

Date _____

Adoration
Giving God praise and honor for who God is as Divine Creator and Lord over all.

Confession
Honestly dealing with sin in your life.

Thanksgiving
Verbalizing what you're grateful for in your life and in the world around you.

Supplication
Praying for the needs of others and yourself.

Requests for myself	Answered
Requests for others	

Your Morning Prayer

Evening Reflection

I'm grateful for...

Three things I want to accomplish tomorrow...

Today's A.C.T.S.

Date _____

Adoration
Giving God praise and honor for who God is as Divine Creator and Lord over all.

Confession
Honestly dealing with sin in your life.

Thanksgiving
Verbalizing what you're grateful for in your life and in the world around you.

Supplication
Praying for the needs of others and yourself.

Requests for myself	Answered
Requests for others	

Your Morning Prayer

Evening Reflection

I'm grateful for...

Three things I want to accomplish tomorrow...

Today's A.C.T.S.

Date _____

Adoration
Giving God praise and honor for who God is as Divine Creator and Lord over all.

Confession
Honestly dealing with sin in your life.

Thanksgiving
Verbalizing what you're grateful for in your life and in the world around you.

Supplication
Praying for the needs of others and yourself.

Requests for myself	Answered
Requests for others	

Your Morning Prayer

Evening Reflection
I'm grateful for...

Three things I want to accomplish tomorrow...

Today's A.C.T.S.

Date _____

Adoration
Giving God praise and honor for who God is as Divine Creator and Lord over all.

Confession
Honestly dealing with sin in your life.

Thanksgiving
Verbalizing what you're grateful for in your life and in the world around you.

Supplication
Praying for the needs of others and yourself.

Requests for myself	Answered
Requests for others	

Your Morning Prayer

Evening Reflection

I'm grateful for...

Three things I want to accomplish tomorrow...

Today's A.C.T.S.

Date _____

Adoration
Giving God praise and honor for who God is as Divine Creator and Lord over all.

Confession
Honestly dealing with sin in your life.

Thanksgiving
Verbalizing what you're grateful for in your life and in the world around you.

Supplication
Praying for the needs of others and yourself.

Requests for myself	Answered
Requests for others	

Your Morning Prayer

Evening Reflection
I'm grateful for...

Three things I want to accomplish tomorrow...

Today's A.C.T.S.

Date _____

Adoration
Giving God praise and honor for who God is as Divine Creator and Lord over all.

Confession
Honestly dealing with sin in your life.

Thanksgiving
Verbalizing what you're grateful for in your life and in the world around you.

Supplication
Praying for the needs of others and yourself.

Requests for myself	Answered

Requests for others	

Your Morning Prayer

Evening Reflection

I'm grateful for...

Three things I want to accomplish tomorrow...

Today's A.C.T.S.

Date _____

Adoration
Giving God praise and honor for who God is as Divine Creator and Lord over all.

Confession
Honestly dealing with sin in your life.

Thanksgiving
Verbalizing what you're grateful for in your life and in the world around you.

Supplication
Praying for the needs of others and yourself.

Requests for myself	Answered

Requests for others	

Your Morning Prayer

Evening Reflection

I'm grateful for...

Three things I want to accomplish tomorrow...

Today's A.C.T.S.

Date _____

Adoration
Giving God praise and honor for who God is as Divine Creator and Lord over all.

Confession
Honestly dealing with sin in your life.

Thanksgiving
Verbalizing what you're grateful for in your life and in the world around you.

Supplication
Praying for the needs of others and yourself.

Requests for myself	Answered
Requests for others	

Your Morning Prayer

Evening Reflection
I'M GRATEFUL FOR...

THREE THINGS I WANT TO ACCOMPLISH TOMORROW...

Today's A.C.T.S.

Date _____

Adoration
Giving God praise and honor for who God is as Divine Creator and Lord over all.

Confession
Honestly dealing with sin in your life.

Thanksgiving
Verbalizing what you're grateful for in your life and in the world around you.

Supplication
Praying for the needs of others and yourself.

Requests for myself	Answered
Requests for others	

Your Morning Prayer

Evening Reflection

I'm grateful for...

Three things I want to accomplish tomorrow...

Today's A.C.T.S.

Date _____

Adoration
Giving God praise and honor for who God is as Divine Creator and Lord over all.

Confession
Honestly dealing with sin in your life.

Thanksgiving
Verbalizing what you're grateful for in your life and in the world around you.

Supplication
Praying for the needs of others and yourself.

Requests for myself	Answered
Requests for others	

Your Morning Prayer

Evening Reflection
I'm grateful for...

Three things I want to accomplish tomorrow...

Today's A.C.T.S.

Date _____

Adoration
Giving God praise and honor for who God is as Divine Creator and Lord over all.

Confession
Honestly dealing with sin in your life.

Thanksgiving
Verbalizing what you're grateful for in your life and in the world around you.

Supplication
Praying for the needs of others and yourself.

Requests for myself	Answered

Requests for others	

Your Morning Prayer

Evening Reflection
I'm grateful for...

Three things I want to accomplish tomorrow...

Today's A.C.T.S.

Date _____

Adoration
Giving God praise and honor for who God is as Divine Creator and Lord over all.

Confession
Honestly dealing with sin in your life.

Thanksgiving
Verbalizing what you're grateful for in your life and in the world around you.

Supplication
Praying for the needs of others and yourself.

Requests for myself	Answered

Requests for others

Your Morning Prayer

Evening Reflection

I'm grateful for...

THREE THINGS I WANT TO ACCOMPLISH TOMORROW...

Today's A.C.T.S.

Date _____

Adoration
Giving God praise and honor for who God is as Divine Creator and Lord over all.

Confession
Honestly dealing with sin in your life.

Thanksgiving
Verbalizing what you're grateful for in your life and in the world around you.

Supplication
Praying for the needs of others and yourself.

Requests for myself	Answered
Requests for others	

Your Morning Prayer

Evening Reflection

I'm grateful for...

Three things I want to accomplish tomorrow...

Today's A.C.T.S.

Date _____

Adoration
Giving God praise and honor for who God is as Divine Creator and Lord over all.

Confession
Honestly dealing with sin in your life.

Thanksgiving
Verbalizing what you're grateful for in your life and in the world around you.

Supplication
Praying for the needs of others and yourself.

Requests for myself	Answered
Requests for others	

Your Morning Prayer

Evening Reflection
I'm grateful for...

Three things I want to accomplish tomorrow...

Today's A.C.T.S.

Date _____

Adoration
Giving God praise and honor for who God is as Divine Creator and Lord over all.

Confession
Honestly dealing with sin in your life.

Thanksgiving
Verbalizing what you're grateful for in your life and in the world around you.

Supplication
Praying for the needs of others and yourself.

Requests for myself	Answered

Requests for others	

Your Morning Prayer

Evening Reflection

I'm grateful for...

Three things I want to accomplish tomorrow...

Today's A.C.T.S.

Date _____

Adoration

Giving God praise and honor for who God is as Divine Creator and Lord over all.

Confession

Honestly dealing with sin in your life.

Thanksgiving

Verbalizing what you're grateful for in your life and in the world around you.

Supplication

Praying for the needs of others and yourself.

Requests for myself	Answered
Requests for others	

Your Morning Prayer

Evening Reflection
I'm grateful for...

Three things I want to accomplish tomorrow...

Today's A.C.T.S.

Date _____

Adoration
Giving God praise and honor for who God is as Divine Creator and Lord over all.

Confession
Honestly dealing with sin in your life.

Thanksgiving
Verbalizing what you're grateful for in your life and in the world around you.

Supplication
Praying for the needs of others and yourself.

Requests for myself	Answered

Requests for others	

Your Morning Prayer

Evening Reflection

I'm grateful for...

Three things I want to accomplish tomorrow...

Today's A.C.T.S.

Date _____

Adoration
Giving God praise and honor for who God is as Divine Creator and Lord over all.

Confession
Honestly dealing with sin in your life.

Thanksgiving
Verbalizing what you're grateful for in your life and in the world around you.

Supplication
Praying for the needs of others and yourself.

Requests for myself	Answered
Requests for others	

Your Morning Prayer

Evening Reflection
I'm grateful for...

Three things I want to accomplish tomorrow...

Today's A.C.T.S.

Date _____

Adoration
Giving God praise and honor for who God is as Divine Creator and Lord over all.

Confession
Honestly dealing with sin in your life.

Thanksgiving
Verbalizing what you're grateful for in your life and in the world around you.

Supplication
Praying for the needs of others and yourself.

Requests for myself	Answered
Requests for others	

Your Morning Prayer

Evening Reflection

I'm grateful for...

Three things I want to accomplish tomorrow...

Today's A.C.T.S.

Date _____

Adoration
Giving God praise and honor for who God is as Divine Creator and Lord over all.

Confession
Honestly dealing with sin in your life.

Thanksgiving
Verbalizing what you're grateful for in your life and in the world around you.

Supplication
Praying for the needs of others and yourself.

Requests for myself	Answered
Requests for others	

Your Morning Prayer

Evening Reflection

I'M GRATEFUL FOR...

THREE THINGS I WANT TO ACCOMPLISH TOMORROW...

Today's A.C.T.S.

Date _____

Adoration
Giving God praise and honor for who God is as Divine Creator and Lord over all.

Confession
Honestly dealing with sin in your life.

Thanksgiving
Verbalizing what you're grateful for in your life and in the world around you.

Supplication
Praying for the needs of others and yourself.

Requests for myself	Answered
Requests for others	

Your Morning Prayer

Evening Reflection

I'm grateful for...

Three things I want to accomplish tomorrow...

Today's A.C.T.S.

Date _____

Adoration
Giving God praise and honor for who God is as Divine Creator and Lord over all.

Confession
Honestly dealing with sin in your life.

Thanksgiving
Verbalizing what you're grateful for in your life and in the world around you.

Supplication
Praying for the needs of others and yourself.

Requests for myself	Answered
Requests for others	

Your Morning Prayer

Evening Reflection
I'm grateful for...

Three things I want to accomplish tomorrow...

Today's A.C.T.S.

Date _____

Adoration
Giving God praise and honor for who God is as Divine Creator and Lord over all.

Confession
Honestly dealing with sin in your life.

Thanksgiving
Verbalizing what you're grateful for in your life and in the world around you.

Supplication
Praying for the needs of others and yourself.

Requests for myself	Answered

Requests for others	

Your Morning Prayer

Evening Reflection

I'm grateful for...

Three things I want to accomplish tomorrow...

Today's A.C.T.S.

Date _____

Adoration
Giving God praise and honor for who God is as Divine Creator and Lord over all.

Confession
Honestly dealing with sin in your life.

Thanksgiving
Verbalizing what you're grateful for in your life and in the world around you.

Supplication
Praying for the needs of others and yourself.

Requests for myself	Answered

Requests for others	

Your Morning Prayer

Evening Reflection

I'm grateful for...

Three things I want to accomplish tomorrow...

Today's A.C.T.S.

Date _____

Adoration
Giving God praise and honor for who God is as Divine Creator and Lord over all.

Confession
Honestly dealing with sin in your life.

Thanksgiving
Verbalizing what you're grateful for in your life and in the world around you.

Supplication
Praying for the needs of others and yourself.

Requests for myself	Answered

Requests for others	

Your Morning Prayer

Evening Reflection

I'm grateful for...

Three things I want to accomplish tomorrow...

Today's A.C.T.S.

Date _____

Adoration

Giving God praise and honor for who God is as Divine Creator and Lord over all.

Confession

Honestly dealing with sin in your life.

Thanksgiving

Verbalizing what you're grateful for in your life and in the world around you.

Supplication

Praying for the needs of others and yourself.

Requests for myself	Answered
Requests for others	

Your Morning Prayer

Evening Reflection

I'm grateful for...

Three things I want to accomplish tomorrow...

Today's A.C.T.S.

Date _____

Adoration
Giving God praise and honor for who God is as Divine Creator and Lord over all.

Confession
Honestly dealing with sin in your life.

Thanksgiving
Verbalizing what you're grateful for in your life and in the world around you.

Supplication
Praying for the needs of others and yourself.

Requests for myself	Answered
Requests for others	

Your Morning Prayer

Evening Reflection

I'm grateful for...

Three things I want to accomplish tomorrow...

It's time to reorder.

Today's A.C.T.S.

Date _____

Adoration
Giving God praise and honor for who God is as Divine Creator and Lord over all.

Confession
Honestly dealing with sin in your life.

Thanksgiving
Verbalizing what you're grateful for in your life and in the world around you.

Supplication
Praying for the needs of others and yourself.

Requests for myself	Answered
Requests for others	

Your Morning Prayer

Evening Reflection
I'm grateful for...

Three things I want to accomplish tomorrow...

Today's A.C.T.S.

Date _____

Adoration
Giving God praise and honor for who God is as Divine Creator and Lord over all.

Confession
Honestly dealing with sin in your life.

Thanksgiving
Verbalizing what you're grateful for in your life and in the world around you.

Supplication
Praying for the needs of others and yourself.

Requests for myself	Answered

Requests for others	

Your Morning Prayer

Evening Reflection
I'm grateful for...

Three things I want to accomplish tomorrow...

Today's A.C.T.S.

Date _____

Adoration
Giving God praise and honor for who God is as Divine Creator and Lord over all.

Confession
Honestly dealing with sin in your life.

Thanksgiving
Verbalizing what you're grateful for in your life and in the world around you.

Supplication
Praying for the needs of others and yourself.

Requests for myself	Answered
Requests for others	

Your Morning Prayer

Evening Reflection
I'm grateful for...

Three things I want to accomplish tomorrow...

Today's A.C.T.S.

Date _____

Adoration
Giving God praise and honor for who God is as Divine Creator and Lord over all.

Confession
Honestly dealing with sin in your life.

Thanksgiving
Verbalizing what you're grateful for in your life and in the world around you.

Supplication
Praying for the needs of others and yourself.

Requests for myself	Answered
Requests for others	

Your Morning Prayer

Evening Reflection

I'm grateful for...

Three things I want to accomplish tomorrow...

Today's A.C.T.S.

Date _____

Adoration
Giving God praise and honor for who God is as Divine Creator and Lord over all.

Confession
Honestly dealing with sin in your life.

Thanksgiving
Verbalizing what you're grateful for in your life and in the world around you.

Supplication
Praying for the needs of others and yourself.

Requests for myself	Answered
Requests for others	

Your Morning Prayer

Evening Reflection
I'm grateful for...

Three things I want to accomplish tomorrow...

Today's A.C.T.S.

Date _____

Adoration
Giving God praise and honor for who God is as Divine Creator and Lord over all.

Confession
Honestly dealing with sin in your life.

Thanksgiving
Verbalizing what you're grateful for in your life and in the world around you.

Supplication
Praying for the needs of others and yourself.

Requests for myself	Answered
Requests for others	

Your Morning Prayer

Evening Reflection

I'm grateful for...

Three things I want to accomplish tomorrow...

Made in the USA
Middletown, DE
04 September 2024

60266047R00106